A Cherry Street Publication

First published in the United States of America by
Secret Compartment, LLC

Cover Art and Layout by RD Larson
Printed and Bound by Lulu.

International Standard Book Number(s) granted in a printing agreement with Lulu
Press, Inc.

Library of Congress Cataloguing-in-Publication Data

Spinoff, The. Volume 1. Issue 1. / edited by RD Larson
eBook - Pages cm. – (Digital humanities)
Includes bibliographical references.
ISBN 978-*-*****-***-* (printed on acid-free paper)
1. Communication in learning and scholarship-Publication strategies. 2.
Scholarly electronic publishing.
3. Humanities-Creative Writing. 4. Humanities-Research. 5. Humanities-
Writing for mass media.

2016   2015   2014   2013   4 3 2 1

This work is a compilation of College of St. Scholastica student submissions. In
fictional submissions, the literary perceptions and insights are based on the
experiences of students, though all names, characters, places, and incidents are
products of author imagination or are used fictitiously. Non-fictional submissions are
written in accordance with the College of St. Scholastica's anti-plagiarism policies and
best practices.

Product or corporate names may be trademarks or registered trademarks, and are
used only for identification and explanation without intent to infringe.

Cherry Street Publishing
An imprint of Secret Compartment, LLC
1200 Kenwood Avenue
Tower Room 4407 – Science Studio 1132
Duluth, MN 55811

✣

Getting into collecting precious metals is a way to accomplish many important things at once. It is more than a hobby. It can be a lot of fun. A big reason why it is fun is because it also takes skill, intelligence, creativity, and respect. It allows one to consider many important aspects of life.

The following guide is intended to allow the reader to consider the joy of precious metals collecting as a practical philosophy. This is not an ordinary guide with difficult to comprehend nonsense about trends and guessing games. This is a real meditation on the nature and substance of currency. But in order to understand the currency collection field, it is often very helpful to consider a quality, real substance. This will become progressively clear.

1. Precious Metals are quality, real substances.

When the reader considers the most precious metals, gold is probably at the top of the list. Gold and platinum, palladium and silver, nickel and copper. These are commonly discussed precious metals. When it comes to nickel and copper, the notion of precious may be a slight overstatement. Still, copper is an incredibly useful material in the world. Use an online encyclopedia to get a quick refresher on the wonders and many applications of copper. Certainly, it is precious, but it is abundant and heavy. These factors all help humans to decide in real-time how precious each metal commodity is by relating the values to global monetary systems. Day to day, each metal has a spot price, which is free and easy to access information provided throughout the world online.

But what is quality? The first tip in this guide is to carefully consider the etymology of the important words the reader encounters in life. What is the essence of *quality,* and how is it measured? This may seem like a waste of time, but considering the essence of quality is fundamental to understanding *value.* Quality and value are often intrinsically linked in the mind of the collector. Meditating on the essence of quality will lead naturally into an even deeper quest to discern the reader's values. Collectors often determine values based on the perceived quality of real substances. This is the basis for most collections and acts of collecting. This tip is a prompting to develop a sense of the use of these kinds of words: quality, value, substance, collection. Use dictionaries, lexicons, and web searches to dig more deeply into key words related to this or any field of personal interest. It is wise to reflect on key words, developing an appreciation for the commonly used works and phrases within any sub-culture. Many use words well, but few have meditated on the power of words as such. Very few realize the words themselves are as strong and even stronger than the materials and concepts they describe.

2. Money is a faith-based system.

For the ease of producing a valuable guide, I would like to defy formal convention and work with you on a more conversational level. I can continue trying to choose words wisely, avoiding pronouns, narrating from a vacuum. But we do not think that way! We prefer a personal guide, an assistant, a partner. Even when we know it isn't real, we enjoy the illusion. Hence, all that annoying western advertising. Everything is geared toward you. You are getting hungry. You need a newer car. You must act now. Et cetera. And when it comes to banking, everyone is lining up to help you. They want to get you to stick your imaginary money in an imaginary computer vault, so they can find arbitrary ways to skim off the imaginary top of your fake paychecks.

Forgive my sudden shift in tone. But this is the truth. You, by working with a bank, are holding up a faith-based system based on absolutely no quality, real substance such as gold or silver. There is no gold or silver 'behind' or 'backing' your money. This is something many people know by now. In fact, as the world has become increasingly cashless and web based, there is literally not even paper cash backing the long chains of 1's and 0's that tell the banks how much money everybody owns. The binary computing code used to represent the paper currencies of the world (which are mostly all *fiat* anyway) is a very persistent illusion. Persistent is the key word here. The illusion may as well be completely real, for the persistence of money is unmatched in its ability to bring human perceptions of pleasure and misery. The illusion of money can bring about the illusion of happiness through material gain. But the loss of currency can be devastating, as it often brings material and personal loss. Real estate is lost over illusions of money.

Behind all that illusion is the substance of faith, which is at least as real as any quality substance.

3. In a world of the real, illusions, and faith...look for the intersections!

Precious metals collection is a way to manage the complexities of currency.

Let's shift from speaking in the abstract to speaking about your own personal situation. What was the first thing you ever did as a child to save money?

How did you learn about saving money?

Though it is bound to change soon as the world continues to abstract its conception of money, most of us can say we learned about saving from a parent or guardian, and it generally involved saving coins and paper in a bank. It is not long, it is said, before kids will think of small piggy banks and metal coins as prehistoric relics.

There is an interesting point here. Many generations have learned the 'value of a dollar' by aligning the symbol of the money to the value of its exchange for real world goods and services. The holder of the non-counterfeit currency is entitled to exchange it in an open market for equivalent goods and services. The holder of the money is not obliged to speak with individual shop owners and service providers about personal ethics, or about how one has come by one's own money. The exchange of money is a pure, philosophical one in its essence. The equation is reduced to its simplest form.

The philosophical exchange is demonstrated as practicality in disguise. In order to establish a necessarily believable agreement among practical persons, the money used in the exchange must hold value equal to goods or services rendered. Why, if not for this, working men and women everywhere would have to concede they have been fooled by a con game of false currency, and unethically stripped of their valuables.

In time, silver and gold became widely understood as valuable by the masses. Their rarity, desirability, their physical and practical applications rendered them a commodity. They could be accurately weighted, formed into coin and bullion, stamped, and reliably accounted for using paper records systems. These are merely facts about the intrinsic, real value of the metals themselves. Their potential as currencies, given the mass perception of these materials, was refined and filtered through the collective consciousness of the entire world. And though the world banking systems, cultures, companies and political systems have all distorted the pure philosophy of currency for myriad agendas, there still exists a world trade of the same pure and precious metals. That ancient trade is still remarkably open and free for much of the world. From Perth Mint in Australia to PAMP in Switzerland, the business of providing pure precious metal in actuality is alive.

4. Saving is a prime motive for considering precious metals.

Saving money is perhaps a more ethical description of the process at hand. Some people are collecting precious metals just to have a hobby, and it can be a very rewarding hobby. Perhaps the most widely practiced hobby of all time is the act of collecting. How many of us have aunts and uncles who have obtained, over the years, an extensive collection of bottle caps? Postage stamps? Cards, pictures, books, on and on. People are collectors. They are some of them hoarders, in deed.

Shopping is linked to collecting. Many collectors are simply people who tremendously enjoy shopping. It is simply that accumulating real property is the consequence of shopping. Do you think some people might prefer shopping and taking possession of things if they knew shortly after their possession, the things themselves would vanish into thin air? I think some people would get tremendous relief from this. If nothing else, there would be far less trash. All that packaging would disappear.

Saving precious metals is a way to experience the joy of shopping, the thrill of taking possession of what the shopping yields, *while* simultaneously saving one's money! Some people would be excellent savers, if only they enjoyed shopping for money!! The desire to save, at a basic level, is the desire to make one's most valuable visions of a happy living take place in some real form or another. Precious metals can be a practical solution for many people who are deeply interested in saving up for real, happy living.

Think: Very few hobbies or collections can be considered as simply putting money away. In fact, many people consider 'saving money' to be the very opposite of shopping, and for this reason they are put off saving money in favor of spending frivolously.

5.   There is such a thing as smart shopping.

The lure of bargains. The rewards of frugality. These can be very powerful when combined with an alignment of shopping and saving. Those who become wise with coupons and food provisions can reap real rewards when it comes to feeding the family.

With the advent of electronic auction websites, and the country filled with lovers and aficionados of precious metals, there are vast sources for finding one's own precious metal collection. There are garage sales, pawn shops, and deep hobby and club organizations throughout the country, with superstars willing to discuss precious metal collection with passion and wisdom. Seek them out! They are much closer than you think, perhaps even your own relation. Most precious meals collectors want you to enjoy it like they do. I have found that collectors are very interesting, with many stories to tell. They are experts. They can see the great and subtle differences in quality, and know a great deal of trivia related to minute details within numismatics and world monetary history.

We can learn so much just by getting a sense of 'what's out there' in the world of precious metals. Be advised: it is easy to get taken up with a faction of precious metals collection that is not really saving in any sense of the word. In other words, there are many ways to be scammed in the realm of precious metals and numismatics. It is going to be helpful to know the ways in which you can be saving as opposed to collecting purely for the experience and novelty.

6. There is a such thing as unintentionally losing money.

The ways in which we can honestly start to come by precious metals is beset all around by scams, counterfeits, and schemes. Partaking in these sideshows can be exciting, and the resulting collections can have great personal appeal. However, we all know that there are people whose old baseball cards were worth fortunes. Because of this, many other baseball card collections were made, and those collections are largely worthless. This illustration is a parable for money, and a highlights a trend we see in nearly every novel industry. An idea is put into motion. It is rarely understood for a time, though it has great merit. Suddenly, it catches on with the masses for what is seen by them as merit. The rare few who had seen the true merit prior to the zeitgeist can truly merit based on their early stake. In this case, old rare baseball cards. It was a good idea to print them. So good, in fact, that after the idea caught on, billions were printed, and the value of the cards diminished. There were once only a scant few cards, and then there were billions of them.

Most things that have been sold in the world have been sold in various degrees of quality. One important aspect of quality is rarity. Some things are only considered to be of utmost quality because of their highest rarity. Original works of art, for example, are priceless if they are genuine, though the reprints of the same original work are cheap. The same is true in the world of precious metals. There is no substitute for real, pure gold and silver. The same is true for copper. There is no other thing even close to copper in the world or on the periodic table.

One of the elegant things about precious metals is their proof of concept. Gold is gold. It is easily verifiable as such. A simple chemical test is all that is needed. This is greatly enhanced and often becomes unnecessary when combined with easy to accumulate common knowledge of numismatics and the industry. Amid all the counterfeits and sideshows and novelties are genuine metals sold by reputable dealers. There are often the most attractive, and easiest to both identify and authenticate. We let the metal do the work of being itself, and we let our understanding of the market guide our decisions to save and sell.

This is a bit more complicated in practice, but the main point is always clear: The value is in the perception of the metal itself. There is some regard for its rarity in form, for instance, if the metal in question is in a limited edition form, or is very old. But by and large, the real value of the collection is in the physical weight of the metal itself. The collection may have all kinds of symbolic or even romantic value. It is possible to buy 'boutique' bars or art bars...pure silver or sterling silver bars commissioned by monarchs and mints throughout the world. They might have special art or symbolism on them, and may be released with special certificates. But an ounce of silver, on any given day, is likely to be perceived as valuable as the market says it is at its spot price. Thius readily available information is always free and circulate d in real time. A collector can easily keep track of the collection's 'fire sale' worth. This simply means that if the collection had to go up for a swift sale, the seller might be able to get the spot value of the collection most quickly and most readily. Think pawn shops, eBay, Craigslist. This is why it is also good to know the collector's community. If you get into some quick need to liquidate part of your collection, you would likely know another precious metals enthusiast who has said at one time, "If you even want to sell or trade, I am interested."

7. The Fire Sale Portfolio

Once you have decided it is persistently interesting, and you are going ahead on the purchase of precious metals, you should make a serious estimation about how much you can realistically save. Notice we say save, and not spend or invest. You are saving. Collecting, perhaps. Somewhere in between saving and collecting. This is true because most collectors are savers and vice versa. In a fire sale situation (and we must always consider the fire sale scenario) each collector informally ranks his or her own treasures by many measures and means. Sentimental value may certainly play a role, here. It is unlikely that a person who is saving and enjoys collecting, who has kept a firm head about the business, would suddenly be in a need position to sell all that has been saved. On several occasions, I have had to sell off parts of my own collection in order to finance home improvements, vacations, and other unexpected (not necessarily unpleasant!) life happenings. This is not sad! Often it is quite the opposite. How fortunate to be in control of one's own finances and valuables that the storms and pleasures of life can be met! I will add that I have not always been able to buy metals at a low price and seel them back at a high price. I have had to sell favored treasures at times when the circumstances of life were even more vital. It is possible to take a monetary loss on the sale of metal, but to still be satisfied with the way the sale mitigated the trajectory of the life event. More about this soon.

The fire sale point of reference is simple. A virtue of the metal is to be able to move it as a currency. While one might truly enjoy and appreciate holding it, it is also very important to employ it as a function of value, to solve problems and render the better things into being. In plain terms, precious metals themselves have been historically attached to a zeitgeist metric, the daily spot chart. At any given moment, one can do a simply bit of math, simply the amount by weight in possession multiplied by current value. A collector can count her collection two ways, thinking about the methods as end points on a spectrum of possible values. The first way, is the more fun way perhaps, the inherited value of one's own collection. What if you were able to present your collection in a game show-like fashion, laying out each item and given the opportunity to relish the story behind each piece? What if you could assign any retail value to your collection?

As an other end of the spectrum figure, we must consider the 'everything must go' value of the very same collection. If you had to part with all of it in a big life decision, what could you safely and quickly expect to get for the whole works? The basic figure here is the weight of everything you've got times the current market spot prices of each metal. This may be tough to hear. If you collect PAMP bullion bars, for example, these bars are often bought at a premium because they are considered an art form. They are highly collectible, and have many limited releases. They are serial numbered, and for this reason they are easy to identify and authenticate. One of their most popular bars is a simple serial numbered, sealed ounce of silver. It is not uncommon to find this simple, flagship bar selling at ten or twelve dollars over its spot value. If the spot price of silver is 25 dollars per ounce, these particular bars may sell on eBay for upwards of $40. This usually works both ways on auction. If you are selling a few of these bars on auction, say three of them at a current spot price of 25 dollars, you may easily sell them at more than $100. Their silver value is only $75, but since you have taken good pictures of them, and kept them in good condition, perhaps they are sequentially numbered and you offer free shipping. You should have no problem selling them for over $100.

Once you sell, and have offered free shipping, you must, of course, pay out of pocket to ship the bars. You eat the cost of shipping, and because you are a small time collector, you'll like pay full retail for any shipping supplies and postage on items at the Post Office. And if you are like millions of other small time buyers and sellers on eBay, you'll also pay 7-10% to eBay and 2-5% to PayPal. This may seem rough, but you are paying for the privilege of reaching the world's market! You are able to find a seller and move the metal to that seller using the most sophisticated selling and shipping platforms ever known to humankind. It may cost you around 20% of the retail sale price just to pack it up, ship it out, and pay the electronic banking and storefront wizards. This is why even when you buy those high end art bars form PAMP and Perth, you can easily still end up clearing 'spot net cash in hand'. In one way, this is a conservative way to look at saving precious metals. If you invest in the industry's better coin and bullion products, you can ensure that your collection will at least yield the current spot value of the metals after all associated selling costs are mitigated.

8. The real value of your treasure is often somewhere within fun and easy to determine High-Low figures.

For the Low figures, think spot prices, or even slightly below spot if you are dealing with a pawn shop. It is quicker and easier to move precious metals at a pawn shop than nearly any other good, but then again pawn shops are not often regarded as the best place to sell!

For the High figures, determine the price you would put on each of your products to display at a trade show. What would your *Buy it Now* prices be, especially if you weren't all that interested in selling your treasures? Remember, strangers are not sentimentally attached to your stuff like you are...but they can become so! That is where the savvy sellers can have opportunities to be profitable well beyond fire sale estimates.

Depending on your motivations and time constraints for selling, you can expect to take in a net cash amount some where in your High-Low range. In the relatively stable and predictable copper market, your holdings cash value is not wildly fluctuating day to day. In gold and silver, however, you can expect your holdings value to fluctuate with the markets.

Think about selling half your collection to an eager market while the spot price was at a two year high. This is fun to think about, especially if you bought it earlier at a two year low. Fun times. There is something to be said about making money on the tides of the market. It is even more rewarding to do this when the reason for converting metal into cash is for a happy life experience, like a vacation. You would have satisfaction knowing you bought something valuable, then sold it for a positive return on investment in order to pay for a life affirming time. This is perhaps a best case scenario. This is also difficult for most collectors to do, as it takes time to become a part of the market, to have a vested interest. Most people invest over time, and so they are subject to the market price of the metals. Those who became interested in collecting in late 2011 and 2012, for instance, likely bought metals while they were at an all time high price. This made selling that metal a losing proposition in 2013 and 2014. It isn't until a collector has amassed samples from a long string of market periods that he or she would become less subject to its ebbs and flows. By collecting throughout a longer period of time, your personal average purchase price index approaches the market average price index. This means you can temper the times you've purchased gold at a high price with the times you've bought it at a lower price.

The spot price at a time when you need or want to sell is more likely to be near the average cost of your purchases. And in the long term, precious metals have consistently retained or grown in their value. This means historically, it has been good to hang on to metals collections for as long as possible.

And now for something completely different…

✤

The various excerpts in this book may not seem well organized at first. This is a small sampling of various thoughts, ideas, and stories pertaining to a much larger endeavor at work in our world today. The point of these texts will seem elusive to many readers. Others will find an intrinsic idea emerging from the pages.

A question is being posed: What is the object of the Holy Spirit? Is it at work in this text? Is it working around you? Is it at work within you?

One of the most widely used and enticing words today is 'Quest'. It seems that every curious person today is on some sort of quest. On the quest, bits of information become clues, and everyday endeavors become adventures. People become heroes and villains. There are untold secrets to discover, and missions to accomplish. These classical ideas are hard to resist. It seems as though the 'Quest' is something we all long for.

This book, like so many others, has been created to pull you into a Quest.

Let it begin.

There you are. Right on time. You found this strange little book among millions of others. How did you get this book? This is not a best seller. It is not widely available. There are many books that start like this. They refer to their readers as 'you'. They are seductive in nature. They eventually tell you that 'it is no mistake that this book found its way into your hands'. And if you read on long enough, they'll tell you that you're God. They'll tell you that you're co-creating the universe with God, and that there is absolutely nothing to fear. They tell you that you are just as capable of writing prophecy and scriptures as the Holy Bible's authors.

You are on a quest, and it is no mistake that you are reading this book. But there is much to fear. People know how to LIE. There are absolutely phenomenal liars in this world. In fact, the king of this world is the greatest liar of all.

3

There are many paths, but they do not all lead to the same place. You must sharpen your faith. You must learn to discern between the truth and the lies. If you want a Quest, why not quest for truth? Some books say there are many truths, or that there are no real truths. LIES. All Lies.

In the end, this book may contain lies. It's only fair to tell you now. But one thing redeems it, and, ultimately, its readers. This entire text has been created for a few important reasons. First and most importantly, it is here for you now, to give you one invaluable piece of advice:

Get a Bible.
The Holy Bible is your greatest weapon. Arm yourself. It will provide you with everything you will ever need on your quest for truth. Without it, you are lost. Without it, there is no quest.
The rest is simply an attempt to open your eyes to the Holy Spirit Project. On the quest ahead, you will see what it s building toward. Ultimately, there is a Worldwide Movement happening. There is a rescue mission to be accomplished. And, if you wish, you will be a part of it.

The rest of this is hope that you will see for yourself.

The rest is only hope that help finds you...
good luck on your quest.

As I sit here at my state of the art computer system and reflect on the events of 2004, I am extremely grateful and happy to be alive and healthy and living as I am tonight. I have my problems; I have my ongoing bouts with sin. I have my blessings, which I certainly abuse. I have my moments of inspiration, which I certainly neglect. I have my ups and downs...my heres and theres. I am lucky. I am blessed. I feel cursed some nights. I feel moments of grave uncertainty. I feel ashamed. I feel afraid.

I read a Viggo Mortensen interview a while back, and in one part he said that he woke up every day when he was in his mid twenties with the overwhelming feeling that he was going to die. And I feel the same way often times. Maybe it's this age. Maybe there's a universal feeling of doom and impending judgement in the hearts of young men who've tested their limits.

I am reading the Bible...or a derivation of it. I am so happy to have this desire and I seek the discipline to finish it...reading from one cover to the other. I am starting now to read Leviticus. I've read through Genesis and Exodus, and I want to dedicate a portion of my fleeting and wasted time reflecting on the journey through these books.

Genesis...It is a fast paced jaunt through the dawn of man. I have a hard time distinguishing if it is in deed the journey of every man...or the Jewish man...or the idea of man. I would like to think that it is my family tree, too. My ancestry...that I came from these words as much as any Jew or Middle Easterner. But with that comes accepting that we, as a species, came from extreme darkness and confusion. We were crazy and ridiculous...and probably haven't come very far from that darkness.

I was struck when I read that Lot's daughters decided to get him drunk and sleep with him in the cave outside the post-apocalyptic Sodom and Gomorrah...this after their Mother turns to salt and they narrowly escape death by divine intervention. We were so nuts that these women thought it best to sleep with their Dad.

Of course there are moments in the Bible when I didn't know what to think over and over. Joseph's brothers went on a very methodical killing spree when their sister was raped and treated like a whore. Isaac and Abraham and right on down the line...these men were quick to call their wives their sisters to get out of sticky situations. And everyone is related to each other. People were sleeping with their half sisters and uncles and cousins...

But then through all of this, God appears to be sifting through humanity wracking His brain to try and create something worth a damn.

He wants to save us, one of us...any of us. He wipes us out...he gets pissed...he gets jealous...he tries plan B and C and D. It's exceedingly difficult. He thinks about giving up on all of us time and again. He hands down laws....he works with flawed man time after time.

And God seems to me to be an alien in a ship, coming down in a cloud to speak with a few flawed men here and there. I know to a great degree I try to box God into my own working understanding. And of course, I can't hold Him in there. I think to myself at times that God and I could work well together, especially in that era, but then I know I'm just as nuts and stupid as any of the forefathers.

It is hard to look back at the early humans and think of them as precious. We're crazy...misguided...hellbent on blaming anything and anyone....constantly forgetting deliverance....complaining....screwing up our lives over and over...

Genesis takes me through the stories I've heard through life. And an anticipation is building already for the New Testament...although it's so far away from this point in my journey.

And Exodus comes in, and It's a long story of the deliverance of the Jews from Egypt. Again, it's somewhat difficult not ask if the Jews and I are linked. If I'm supposed to accept that these people are embedded in my genetic code...I don't look like them...I have never been to their home. I have never participated in their ceremonies. For those men today that can trace their roots genealogically back to these people, I hope they embrace who they are. I make allowances in my life...I think 'maybe have them in me'. Maybe that's part of the stuff I have to start transcending now. Transcend race...time...color...geography...tradition...heritage....all of it.

And that is a little difficult. I think 'Is it okay that I call this God my own?' After all, Egypt...the Vikings...the Romans...the Greeks...they all had their own gods. And then there's this one from the Bible who helps and sees over the Jews from such a long time ago. Is it okay for me to forsake all the rest, and go with this one? Where was the 'me' of that day? In caves? The Germanic tribes were somewhere in another part of the world, set apart from the Jews. But I don't know this for sure. A big part of getting into the Bible is accepting that it can be mine. That God from then, incessantly instructing Moses about how to build the lampstand and the chest and the tent and al; the gold veneered stuff and the purple and scarlet stuff...is that my God, too? Would the Jews have let me tag along out of Egypt with them? Would God have let me go, too? Aaron was set apart as the minister of God to all the people out there eating Manna...would I have found the Manna? Would Aaron preach to me? Would I have trusted any of these people?

The bottom line is I want to accept it all, as far away as I am from it today. I want this all to fill my heart and teach me, so that 2000 pages later when Jesus pops up, and finally extends these words to the Gentiles, I can own up to salvation. I don't want to be a tagalong-- Clutching to someone else's history and God because I am so lost to have found the one created for me.

But I can accept that my ancestors were Godless. Maybe. My grandpa seems Godless. He beat up my Dad. To hell with going back two thousand years or more...all I have to do is go back 30.

So...back to Exodus. We get caught up at the end of it and into the beginning of Leviticus with these repetitive, thorough instructions on how to build this dwelling place for God. And the Jews are out there eating manna and worshiping whatever comes along...golden calves...etc. God is meanwhile instructing Moses and Aaron on how to cut up and burn the animals in a pleasing way. What to do with the guts and the fat of the animals. How to bake the bread without yeast. How to wear their hats and gold and how to build the tent. And I know there's a lot more specifics to come.

I choose to soak it all in, as patiently as I can. I will let my eyes pass over every word. I fall asleep, and my transition from awake to asleep is vivid and filled with things I can't really make sense of, but I can tell I am thinking about this stuff. It is swirling around in my head. I have, for the last few years, been exposed to some pretty startling and troubling imagery in my dreams. However, I am rarely 'scared' for very long by these images. I sometimes think I should be more afraid of what passes through my brain at night. Some of it is completely insane and disturbing. But I get over it quickly.

But the nights I read the Bible and then fall asleep...it is weird. I can't really figure out what is happening, but something is happening. It is a mix of fear and excitement...not really of peace...but it's bearable so far. It's just plain weird. I have to sleep with the light on a lot of times. And I catch myself a couple times most nights somewhere in between sleep and awake. I start to get imagery or almost audible voices and situations while still being a little awake, and I pull awake and open my eyes. It frightens me, and I wish and pray that God can help me find a greater peace in the transition from awake to asleep. I don't dread it, but I shouldn't be this weird. I don't like my mind playing tricks on me. Once I'm asleep, you know, the dreams kick in and weirdness abounds sometimes. But I don't like it kicking in too early. I wish for more comfort and peace.

But I'm a sinner. I'm wrestling with a lot of mental trouble. I think rotten things. I hate that. God knows the problems there.

But then I have such wonderful gifts that off set the mental crap. I have a wonderful life coming together. I have great friendships and strong family ties. I have a completely wonderful girlfriend who I want to marry and start a family with. I pray that God grants me a healthy and long lasting family with Sandi. I want kids and a strong marriage. I want to overcome my mental stresses and focus on the gifts that lie in God's Word and promises.

Going in to this Bible journey, I have a lot of my own baggage and also ideas about what I want out of all this. I guess I should leave it behind. I am interested and afraid of angels. I am interested in the Holy Spirit inspiring what I write and come up with in my exploration. I don't want to twist the Word of God into my own scheme. I have these 'big ideas' about the Lemniscate Agency and finding God in my weird expression. I want to get the me out of all of it, and the Word of God running pure throughout my writing. But then that's why there's a Bible. God doesn't need me writing anything, right? What of this? My journal? My website? My high falutin' ideas of an Agency and Worldwide Rescue? Of Jesus being the Commander of the Angels, and preparing a homecoming for them...of operating under the guise of some pseudo-angel human gatekeeper....what the Hell am I doing, anyway? I confuse myself. Is it Vanity?

Power hunger? Could any of it be a true and Holy calling to put my gifts in God's hands? I truly wish for that and only that. I don't want to be a devil. I am bad, but I don't want that. I want to be a pseudo angel...not for vanity and power....but for real...for love. I want to help out the cause...it's the only thing worth while around here.

Well...I guess I'll go read now. I love you, God. Thank you for the Message...I'll be back to You soon....

The HOLY SPIRIT Project – Taken from Lemniscate Agency Transcripts, 11/2003:

"I was in a car…"

And the car was cruising along the road. We were going about 95 in a 45. There were four cars chasing us. They were two black sedans and two big trucks. One was brown. One was white. They had blue lights in their dashboards. They had loud sirens. Three police vehicles were following them. They were all chasing the car I was in.

The people in this car, even the driver, had done nothing wrong. They were taking me to a place: the top of the State Street Bridge. The people in this car were innocent, good people. I was impressed with the driver's skills. I don't know how he did what he did.

The people chasing the car were chasing me. I am a member of an agency. My agency has been under investigation for many years. It is a large organization. It is in your town. It is doing many things in your town.

I did not believe the war would start as early as it did. But it had started by the time this chase ensued. It was still early, but it had begun.

I have no knowledge of how lose a bunch of cars. I was not capable of being nervous or threatened, but I knew the people in this car were uneasy. The driver was very tense, but he truly believed he could outrun all of the cars and trucks. He did not know that he would be successful. But he would bet on it. He was betting on it for my sake, and in spite of the innocent blood buckled into his car.

I read a particular book everyday. It was given to me by my superior officers. It contained a schedule of daily events and mission work. I was always on assignment. I always read the book. I had to follow the book to the letter. I was not allowed to make mistakes.

I made mistakes all the time. But, as I would continue to read the book handed down by my officers, I would discover that my failures were all part of my training. Every last one of my infractions had been planned for ahead of time. My book and my assignments had never failed to guide me. They had never truly endangered me. All I had to do was follow the book. It took care of the rest.

The book had planned for this chase. This chase was part of my mission. I was supposed to make this all happen. By this point in my time on Earth, I was no longer surprised by a situation such as this. My life had been often threatened by now. I was a warrior. I had seen the beginnings of war. I had been training for years.

The book said to smoke. I had never understood it. But, I took to smoking. After I started smoking, it told me to quit. I did this. And then it told me to start again.

It has been doing this to me for years now.

I suppose it has caused me to meet many people critical to my mission work. There were many cases when it was necessary to interact with people as a smoker. At least, for the ones I was sent to.

I Was a spy. Smoking is a sign of being off the path. The work I did required me to be off the path more then on the path. However, I was never truly off my own path. I just had to follow my book--the ever important training manual, handed down by my superiors.

And we were talking about the war now. It was very important to follow commands. It was very important to do the work. Training was becoming blurred with real work. It was beautiful and tragic. I did not need to understand it. This requirement to stay true to the agency was the hardest thing. It was the only reason many of my fellow agents were no longer with me. I see the struggle in my notes. I am not willing to fail.

The car chase was heating up. Two of the vehicles had made it up alongside our ride. It was intense. Everybody was breathing heavily. They were praying. It was quite wonderful. I love to hear the praying.

There were stories rising. They always did. But these stories were getting difficult to bear. They were hunting our agents. We never had secrets. The ones hunting us knew exactly what to look for. Many of them had been disavowed. I did not believe there would be such a division. It was like the beginning. It was the reason the agency was built.

We were being hunted, and it was easy to identify most of us. We were agents. We were marked as such. We were instructed to wear the clothing of the time. We were allowed to get supplies in the supermalls and department stores. It, too, was training. We knew that the way we had been made was done so for purpose. But to hear stories of the way they were starting to corner us and expose us made me look at some thoughts I could usually force away.

I had known many amazing superiors. They had taught me how to truly live as an agent. They taught me how to see the intricacies of the work. They taught me the power of the truth about the time. I had been given strange work to do, and my path confused me sometimes. I was led into some extremely terrible situations. I had made some awful decisions involving escape and self preservation. My decisions more often proved to be self destruction and dead ends.

But then the book would come again the next morning and make sense of what had been done. Many of the debriefings seemed provocative and sometimes controversial. We questioned the one we worked for more often than not. But this was allowed. Thoughts were always allowed. Just not will.

Rumors were also arising that our agents' thoughts were being read now by the disavowed and by the enemy. Telepathy was a rising sign of the time. Telepathy frightened many of us. We were allowed to be frightened. It did not feel like it must feel for the people, but it made our thoughts race. Many agents were consumed by thought induced paranoia. It was one of my greatest thorns. I was a spy. I had been training for many years to blend in and lie low. I had spent many years developing ties with potential agents, only to discover that they had become suspicious of me. They were concerned with my plans. Of course, I had none. I only had my orders. These potential agents had become resistance instead. The ones I sought to save had also sought to destroy me. We were beginning to meet again in the middle, and this was becoming stressful.

I was told to drink. The work I had been scheduled for involved a lot of drinking and commiserating with the people. This was the brunt of the work. It was nearly all involved with human relations. This work is what had led me to knowing the people in the car with me. These people had become so dedicated to the agency that they were taking risks for us. They followed a completely civilian code and often times would never understand or show interest to join our agents, but they fought for us anyway. It was the sort of blind dedication that we were debriefed about but did not believe in. It was the ultimate misunderstanding between the people and the agency. We could see and they could not. Sight was the reason we fought, but theirs was beautiful blindness.

It didn't matter here. The vehicles were boxing us in. The men chasing us on this road are just like the people with me. They either believe in what they are being told to do, or they believe in themselves above all things. I used to know some of these men personally. They invited me into their homes. They introduced me to their wives. They fed me animals and very nice desserts. We smoked cigarettes and played cards. We exchanged stories about women and almost never about politics and never ever about religion.

And here they were, about to bring me down with the innocents. They were relentless. They were trained for this.

I am supposed to make something amazing happen. This is to be my first display of absolute authority. In these days, and from them on, ours is to be the final authority. We were reluctant to exercise it, for since this all began we had learned about what exactly has been at stake. The training took thousands of years, but looking back, I'd say it was a blink.

It was happening now.

I told the young woman sitting next to me to take off her seatbelt. It was a tough sell. The other men had not been wearing them.

I also told Jeremiah to open the glove box and to get up onto his knees. We were about to hit the State Street bridge. I was going to take the wheel from the backseat and veer off the right as soon as we reached the top. I wound down my window and the sounds of sirens and horns came flooding into the cab. I looked over at the lights and at the expressions of the man as he yelled out at us from the car to the immediate left.

I had been preparing for this moment. I had learned about it 41 days prior. This was something that was absolutely going to happen. It was to be my first display of our authority. This being said, I still had an enormous amount of stressful thought. If I were a normal person, my heart would have exploded and my brain would have been riddled with aneurisms.

We crossed the bridge. The people listened to me. I took the wheel. The car went into the Madison River. The chase ended abruptly. The car came floating down the river. No one was hurt a bit. Nobody said a word for three and a half minutes. There was a car waiting for us five blocks up the river. The car got caught up at a specific location by the shoreline. We entered the new car casually. We all sat in the back and waited to be taken home. We would be debriefed, and the three people with me would become agents on this night. New Seeing Faith. There is nothing else like it.

88

There were a great many orphans in the twentieth century. More than ever. Little children showed up all over the world on doorsteps. Young men and women were picked up while walking the streets. It did not take much to go into an orphanage and take a child home. Often times, nobody knew where these orphans came from. Some of them had peculiarities. This could not be explained by anyone. It was simply accepted and not often discussed. There were many small and peculiar children who arrived here in the twentieth century. The most obvious distinction between these children and everyone else was their absence of sexual anatomy. These children were quickly discovered all around the world by doctors and scientists, young and old. Surprisingly, little was done about this. Very little was said. There were no experiments or research. Each case was handled individually by one or a few people. Of course, there were exceptions to this. Many of the sexless children fell into the hands of morally corrupt people. There were tragedies. There was confusion. But, in the larger way of things, these children were cared for.

As these children grew, they naturally understood some things about themselves. They all knew who they were, and what they were supposed to do. They sought out companionship, and most of them became well educated by schools built by humankind. They learned to speak eloquently. They learned to be comforting. They did their work. They married. They started families. They did this for the agency. They were all agents.

88

The HOLY SPIRIT Project – Agency Release #7 – Destiny and Prayer

You wake up one day, and nothing is ever the same. It has happened many times. It happened when Pearl Harbor was attacked. It happened in New York a short while ago. Although the future is not clear to us, many people are quite sure it will happen again.

Tragedy happens suddenly, as do miracles.
You wake up tomorrow, and life changes for you. It is nothing to fear, nothing to hide from. The future is going to happen.

You are walking down your driveway, and a stranger calls out your name. You look to see who it is, and you are confronted with your destiny.

You are chosen.
You have important work to do for God.

These days are difficult, and heroes are everyday people in difficult times. You are given a list of names. You recognize some of these names. Some of these people are your friends. Some are your family. Some are enemies. Some are completely unfamiliar.

You are enlisted to meet with each one of these people and prepare them for the end of the world. You have to show them that their names are written in a very important book, and that there is a space reserved for them in a very special place. You are not talking philosophically or metaphorically. You've seen this place with your own eyes. You've bent down and touched the ground. You've been taken to it and shown your place.

You are chosen.

You are personally responsible for assuring that the people on your list have had an absolute chance to decide whether or not

13

they are willing to come with you. You are entrusted to show them the way to go home.

The ultimate choice is left to each person on your list. However, you must convince yourself that you've done your best to help, as this is a matter of great consequence. You are not the only way for these people. You are a part of the effort. You are part of the plan. You are part of the agency.

You are chosen.

This is no longer an evangelism. This is not an adventure. This is not a test. This is not a drill. This is life. This is the final countdown.

People are out there right now, ordering their lunches and pumping their gas. They are smoking cigarettes and watching CNN. They are speeding. They are picking their kids up from school. They are crawling over the earth in small, straight lines. Back and forth, back and forth.

You have a duty. How many names? Ten...twenty...two thousand?
Maybe just one. Maybe one is enough.

Let's put it another way.

I am calling you on the telephone, because we are good friends and I have some inside information. Our town is going to be destroyed in one week. There is a craft built and prepared to rescue people from the town. It has supplies. It has wonderful accommodations. It was built for you and I. It's the only thing that will be untouched by the destruction of our town. I am calling you because I know you don't want to be destroyed in one week. And I am offering you a key and directions to the loading dock of this craft. I am dead serious, and the choice is yours. If you wish, you may bring who ever you want. Make a list of the people whose lives you wish to save. Get them all together before the week is over, and bring them to the place I am talking about. I have directions for you, and a key to the entrance. I hope you bring a lot of people with you. We'll have just enough space for them.

As the week is coming to an end, I call you again. I am calling to tell you that the town is not going to be destroyed yet, but it is still not safe. In fact, it's in a very volatile state right now, and it could be destroyed with very short notice. However, because you are my friend, I will give you notice as soon as I can, and you will be responsible for yourself and the lives of the people you wish to save. You should remind the people you've gathered together to be ready to move at a moment's notice. This is a very serious situation, but if you keep your cell phone on, I will be able to get through. When you hear from me again, it will be time. Until then, be alert and take comfort in the fact that you have a place to go when disaster strikes, and you and your loved ones will be safe.

Okay.
Make a list.
Family and friends. Acquaintances. People known.
Everyone I went to school with
Everyone I've ever worked with
Everyone who will listen or believe or has tried to do good once
Everyone who is too stubborn to believe
Oh, God...who is unacceptable?
The list is so long, and I can't be an elitist.
Will I be saved?

I WILL BE SAVED. PRAY THIS.....
I WILL BE SAVED.
It starts with me.
In the name of Jesus Christ, our lord, I am saved.
I am wrapped and blanketed in the power of the Holy Spirit and looked upon with favor and empathy. I am blessed to be a

witness. I have fallen from a great height, and the ascension is long, but I will be saved. I will return to my Father. My Father loves me and has saved me with His grace. I am loved. I am loved. I am loved. My soul is clean. My body is healthy. I am healthy. I am safe. I am beautiful. God says I am beautiful. God is happy that I am saved. I am loved. I am blessed. I have never been closer to God. I will continue to grow in my faith and I will be a light unto the darkness. I will conquer all my demons and my sicknesses. I will triumph in the name of Jesus over anything that invokes fear in me. I am not afraid of untimely death. God has planned for me to journey down this path, and promised me salvation. I have been through the darkness, and still a light shines brightly inside of me that cannot be extinguished with fear, torment, and threat. The devil has tried to trick me. The devil has tried to sicken me and weaken me and steal my soul. But I have triumphed over him. My soul is my own and granted to me by God and protected by God in the name of the Holy Trinity. Jesus is my savior, and as I walk through the darkness, my light burns brightly, now and forever. I am saved. I am loved. There is no disease in my body. There is no trace of the evil inside of me. The evil has gone away. The evil is dead. There is no evil. I am a spiritual warrior, and God has won the battle over my soul. The Devil will run away, for the Devil is weak and cannot claim my body or my mind. My spirit is healing everything in me at this moment. It is most certainly true. There is nothing in me to fear or run from. I cannot lose. I cannot be betrayed again. I am forgiven of my past, and my future is spectacular. I can overcome my fears. The Devil is weak. I am a survivor. I've seen the horror and the deceit and I am tired of it. I will not let it hurt me. I will not let it have power over me. I am a successful spiritual warrior in the name of Jesus. I will win this bloody war. The victors fight with me. I am alive. I am well. I have beauty in my life. I am true. I am right. I am strong. There is nothing in me that can be torn down by the devil. The Devil has gone away. Ignore him. Ignore the evil. The evil cannot hurt me anymore. The evil has gone. The good is here, inside me. This is most certainly true. I have nothing to worry about. I have

trained with God on my side. I am here with God. God is here
with me. Jesus has showed me evidence of the glory of God.
Jesus has come to me personally and worked miracles in my life.
Jesus has not led me into impossible struggles. We have
triumphed. Jesus forgives me for the times I've turned away.
Jesus understands my spiritual battles. Jesus forgives me. Jesus
protects me. Jesus loves me and will resound here in my heart
until the end of time. I am strong. I am healed. I am a valiant
spiritual warrior.

This is most certainly true, and nothing and no one can take this
away from me for any reason ever again.

The HOLY SPIRIT Project: Agent Profiling (Who are they? What's happening?)

"The stillness was driving him insane..."

Every word, every little ridiculous fleeting thought. Every incomplete sentence. Every passing glance. There was nothing satisfying. There was nothing left to be written; nothing left to be done. It was choosing between the dash—the dash and the semicolon. It was choosing the right tense. The tenses were boring. The dashes were overused. Nothing was worth a damn. The time it took to sit down and eek out a few sentences...worth less than the words. The time was worth less than the words.

He refers to himself as him. Or himself. He's creating a platform from which he dives into nothing. It's another sad attempt to perpetuate the nothing. He wants incomplete sentences. He wants obscurity. He wants no one to get it. There is no it. It was existentialism for the dead.

He lived in the stillness. He lived in the place where the others lived, too. And it was normal. It was all falling apart, but there was no alarm. The progression of the doom was calming and expected. The people were scrubbing the neurotoxins into their bloodstream without being reminded. They were eating the poison and drinking the little death a day at a time. There was no way to remind anyone of their fall. There was no way to say a thing to anyone. There was nothing absolutely to be done. It was downward sloping normalcy. There was no way to wake the sleeping. There was way to tire the unrelenting.

He was born for the apocalypse. His soul was created to withstand tragedy. He assumed his increasing insensitivity was perversion and sickness. Darkness was falling; he could pick it up and wield it. When the bodies begin to fall into the dirt, he'll find his strength. When the cries get loud, the trumpets will sound in his heart. When the streets are filled with tears and the churches are filled with sorrowful cries of confused and tormented godless wretches, the business will occupy his mind. He will finally know his purpose. It would not be the fall of man that cripples his spirit. But the stillness in waiting might.

This is a time. There have been other times. There have been so many other times. And there will be times to come. This is a time where no adjective fits. It is not the best or the worst or strange or sad or sick. There is not a worthy thing to say about any of this. This is just another time.

Writing is ridiculous.
The world is crumbling. This is the hope. If the world is not crumbling, is it hardening. It is accustomed to travesty. The end times, they say. The end times. The end times. He has heard this over and over, but so have the people who lived in all the other times. The world is always on the brink. Doomsday is always around the bend. And the cry of the people has always been for relief. But there is something in the air now. There is something that may have always been, but this man is new and merely observing the desperate world. The thing in him which he has mistaken for sickness is echoing in the hearts of many in this time. It is not a cry for relief. It is not a prayer for pity or pardon. It is an outcry for tragedy. It is a desire to see the undoing of the hardening world. The way it breathes...its hideous efficiency...it is tireless and evolving exponentially and it suffocates everything. The world must be stopped. It is amazing. It is fascinating. Never before has it been so easy to identify as awful, yet so easy to accept as inevitable.

He watches his family ties and friendships as they are consumed by invisible fire. And he is not permitted to speak out about what has been instilled in him. All this time, and all this doctrine. It resounds in him as difficult truth. It is safety. It is the only obvious way. Still, it is clouded over and unrecognizable to the world. He cannot evangelize. He cannot speak eloquently enough. His heart will break if it is shown to the ones he loves. His words and thoughts and deeds are

17

halfhearted at best. He is weak. He is conflicted. He is unable to define genuine with anything in his grasp.

He wants to prepare everyone for salvation. But he cannot accept his own. He accepts his own, but cannot accept it. He accepts it, but cannot accept it. He accepts it, but cannot ACCEPT it. HE ACCEPTS IT, but it goes on and on. The sin remains. The deathtrap called earth remains. He is living in the absolute best of it. He is living in the belly. It is oblivion. He is disgusted and disheartened by his thought and written word. It is a part of a language he despises. He understands original sin.

This can go on for 1000 pages, and the time and the energy and the words will be a waste and nothing is readable. Nothing is worthy. Nothing is helping. He cannot help anybody. He feels as though his attempt to quantify and qualify thought is an evil scheme. The voice is corrupt. The tone is fatalist and antagonistic. All he wants to say is that there needs to be salvation. There needs to be a breakdown. There needs to be a separation between the goodness left in us, and the rest. Quick, before there is none left.

He worries that he is the only one who is evil. This comes from him. This is his own sick twist on a relative world.
No. no.no.no.nononon nonon n on n on and on and onnnn
There will be salvation, because it is written. It is WRITTEN. He accepts this, and invites the truth. Let it set it ablaze and set it free. Whenever.

The HOLY SPIRIT Project – Agency Release: Candidate
Testimonial
08/20/03

God can work the miracles and prophecies however it is to be
done. I am not a prophet. I am a seeker and a searcher. I know
nothing about any of this.

I was born into this world, and I have no recollection of what
happened before I was born. All I know about this planet and
our civilization is what I've been taught and exposed to in my 24
years. And I have no concrete idea about what will happen when
I die and leave this planet. All I can imagine, hope, have faith in
and pray for in death are the things I was taught while living
here.

There is a certain attraction in imagining that I know about
things to come in my own lifetime on this planet. I would have
to admit that some of these attractions could be wrong.

I was baptized when I was a baby. I was raised as a Lutheran. I
was raised in the late 20th century in Wisconsin. I am an
American Citizen. My father was in the Army, like his own
father.

When I was being taught my religion, I was taught that people
are sinful, and it is a good idea to be sorry for the sins, and to ask
that they be forgiven. I was taught about a man that lived a long
time ago that was going to come back to Earth and save people
who were sorry for their sins. I was taught that I should be a
morally decent person who is guilty of mortal sins, and that I
should have faith in the man who was coming again. I was
taught that if I believed in him and felt guilty and asked him for
forgiveness, then I would be saved from this planet and I will
have a spot in Heaven.

For a time in my life, I did not believe in sin. But that has changed. I can see that people are sinful. It is not a mystery.

For a time in my life, I did not believe that there was a powerful reason to admit wrongdoing to the man who lived a long time ago. I did not want to accept that apologizing to him and asking him to forgive me was the best thing to do with my life. I did not accept the idea that he was coming back to this planet again to judge everybody and take all his believers to heaven.

For a time in my life, I did not accept that there is a Hell where evil people go forever. I did not understand or like the idea of Hell. But as I grew up, I saw that even if there is not a Hell beyond Earth, there is a Hell on Earth. It is very large and consuming. I understand that I'm not supposed to like the idea of Hell, and it is not in my nature to accept Hell, whether it exists on this Earth or beyond. I am not happy about the Hell I've encountered on Earth with my own senses. And I do not want to be part of it, although I know I am. There are countless things I've experienced here that I would call Hell. And I know that I should be grateful that the Hell I've experienced pales in comparison to depths of the Hell on Earth.

I have taken evil into my body. I have dwelled in it, and I have made jokes about it. I have turned away from morality and responsibility to pursue darkness and premature death. I have understood that the ways to explore evil are endless and seductive. I have actively sought out evil, both knowingly and unknowingly. I have looked at it straight on with complete understanding of its nature, and I have accepted it as my own. I have done this throughout my life. There have been times in my life when I have decided not to accept anything but darkness. And I have decided, after careful consideration, that I am sorry. It was wrong of me to be so careless. And I want to change my ways.

But now, although I do not think human beings are very deserving of something like this, I wish it was true that God was coming down to take people away from here. Some people might think that I am a coward for wanting to escape from the Hell on Earth. But that is exactly what I desire. I want to escape Hell, and take the ones I care about with me. I am old enough to understand that the things I have pursued on Earth are quite often selfish and ridiculous. They lead me into trouble. There have been times when I thought I might not escape the peril I have sought.

There is a book that documents the life of a man who speaks of salvation. He is portrayed to be God's only true son. He is portrayed to be the King of all people. It is written that he is coming back here to do God's work in the final days of life as we know it.

**

In one week, Mars will be the closest it's been to Earth in over 70,000 years. Mars, after the moon, is closer to earth than anything else in space. We do not know very much about what exists on Mars.

It is entirely possible that intelligent life exists on Mars. It is also entirely possible that nothing intelligent exists on Mars. It is likely that absolutely nothing will happen on Mars in a week.

But imagine for a moment that we had the technology on Earth to interact with Mars in some way. Let's say, for instance, that we want to send a shuttle over to Mars, either to explore, or to bring something back to Earth. The best time to do something like this would be in a week, when Earth is so close to Mars. Perhaps it would have been even wiser to calculate how long it would take to catch Mars where it will be in a week and plan accordingly.

Or, perhaps it is good to plan the entire trip so that we use this time when Mars is at its relative closeness, and capitalize on these moments so that the entire trip can be accomplished with respect to the orbits of these two planets. That would mean that by the time Mars is at its closest point to Earth, we would actually be on Mars gathering info or exploring, and we would leave soon after Mars was at it's closest point. We would plan to get Mars before it is closest, leave after it is at closest. That way, our departure and arrival on Earth would be....

Okay, let me say this another way. Let's imagine that there is an important interaction that is to take place between Earth and Mars. Something is supposed to happen. There are three time and space relationships between these two planets. The first is the time when Mars and Earth are getting closer to each other. The second is when Mars and Earth are at their closest point to each other. And the third is when Mars and Earth are getting farther apart.

If we wanted to plan for this interaction, then, the optimal time for the actual interaction would be when the two bodies are closest together. This way the round trip will take place so that the halfway point of the trip is when the two bodies are closest. If the trip is planned any other way, one of the two voyages will be longer than the other.

If we wanted to use this time when Mars is the closest it's been in 70,000 years...we should have been on the way a while ago. We should either be there by now or be arriving shortly. And we should be leaving soon.

Therefore, if for some reason there is intelligent life on Mars, and they had planned an interaction with Earth, the same rules would apply. They should either be here right now, or be arriving shortly, and they should be leaving soon.

It probably seems outlandish for me to consider any of these possibilities at length.

But what if God's angels or even Jesus was living on Mars right now? What if they have been planning to come to Earth since the time Jesus was here before? What if these times on Earth are the end times, and Jesus is coming back to save his believers right now, in these very moments?

How would the believers find out about this? And how would all that salvation business work?

Of course, I have no idea about the mind or plans of God. But it is written that Jesus will come again. My mind is naturally inquisitive, and I seek to understand God in a real way. I am not completely satisfied by whimsy and the ideas that God is not logical and His plan is not conceivable.

I think that, at the very least, human beings will be able to understand what has happened right after Jesus comes here and saves believers. That is, if there's anybody around to understand. Theories will fly all over. Scientists will write about it and offer explanations. Artists will recreate the events. History will be recorded, and hindsight will be 20/20.

But right now, before he has come, the news is not flooded with theories and ideas about this prophesied event. And I feel apprehensive to write about it because it might be easy to draw conclusions that I am trying to spin what is unclear into something I am comfortable with.

So, I say again, I have no idea what I'm talking about. I'm just writing. I have absolutely nothing to gain except continued fascination for my search. Absolutely, I seek salvation. And I want it so much that I am willing to let my imagination run, and I am willing to consider far away possibilities of how God might return.

The idea of rescue is stunning to me. And my soul, or at least my critical thinking skills imagination, cry out for truth. I do not believe it is acceptable for me to sit back and wait for God to knock on my door and provide me with salvation. Instead, I believe in seeking, knocking, and crying out for God to show the way to be saved. I do believe that there is nothing I can do to earn salvation, and I am willing to accept that I have searched in all the wrong places and that I am not close to finding what I am looking for.

Still, a part of me sits at a computer in the middle of the night typing and pondering this concept of salvation. I consider the history of my religion and how it reached my young heart. I consider the state of the world. I understand that the world became round 500 years ago, electric 100 years ago, and digital 20 years ago; and that tomorrow is alive with possibilities of things we won't understand until they've come to pass. I also understand that for each of these turning points in the world, there was a dreamer who saw it coming, other dreamers who saw alternatives, and skeptics and persecutors who refuted vigorously every part of every dream along the way.

I dream about salvation becoming something so real we can reach out and touch it. I dream about people rejoicing in the truth because it has arrived as promised. I know that I might be dreaming about things that will never be. There are many who have dreamed of exactly the same thing in their time, only to pass down their faith and accept fate.

As time goes on, I find peace in what has been written. I find hope in my aspirations of what is to come. And I am happy to accept my role in this place as a humble seeker and conflicted human. I seek truth and life and salvation. I am sick and tired of the stupid evil things. I can see that they're not going to leave without force. I pray for direction, guidance, and lasting peace.

Forgive me. Teach me. Accept me. We'll see.

The HOLY SPIRIT Project – **AGENCY LEMNISCATE** Letter
from a Friend
circa. 2003

I've written this letter to eventually call a meeting. I hope that
the meeting is a time when Christian men and women who are
truly seeking God come together and feel free.

I am undertaking what I would like to call mission work. I do
not know anything about its significance or validity. I know that
I will be approaching issues that, to me, are heavy and
important. I pledge to be honest with my mission work from
this moment on. I will state what I believe it to be as carefully as
I can. I will leave it all open to anyone who finds it interesting or
worthwhile in their pursuits.

I hope that the letters I write will engage Christians and non-
Christians in thought and debate. I hope that these thought
create progress in our time.

I only know that these moments are ours. If you are reading this,
you share in these moments with me. As I write this, I am a
young and hopeful man. I am hopeful that I can be saved from
my darkness in a way that leaves no doubt in my being that I am
free and completely safe. I wish away my darkness, and the
darkness of those who also wish it away.

I am calling my mission the Lemniscate work. Lemniscate is the
symbol for infinity. I am seeking salvation, which I believe has a
direct correlation to eternal life. I am seeking infinity. I am
seeking God, and I believe the way to him is through His Son. I
have looked into the religions of the world. I confess I don't
know much about any of the religions I've studied. I am young,
and lots of people know more than me about any given subject.

I have the beginnings of a plan. The plan, I hope, is not my own.

Let me put it a better way. The beauty and power of the plan, if there is any, is not mine. It is God's. And all of the flaws and imperfections and potential sin that can come of it is not God's. I am unclear about the separation between mankind, sin, and the Devil. But I know there is a connection between us all. And God is the way out of the cycle of being a sinner, a human, or being connected in any way to the Devil.

This being said, I encourage anyone who finds any part of my mission to be dark or demeaning to Christian principles to speak boldly in their own voice against mine. I hope to God that I do not create separation between anyone and their connection to God. I do want to trigger questions and thoughts that lead to a better and more meaningful relationship with Him.

I am young and probably unqualified to do what I am doing. I am only trying to get closer. I want more than this, whatever this is tonight. I don't want to be greedy. I'm just thirsty. I want lots of faith, and I want to know why I believe what I do.

I hope you do, too.
PART TWO
(more interesting)

Based on the Gospel of Matthew, as well as the other hundreds of references to Angels in the Bible, I am very curious about the Celestial. It is written that Jesus Christ will return to this Earth, and that when He does, it's going to be a pretty big deal. It is also written that when He does come, He will be assisted by God's angels. There will be a lot of them. This is a key concept for me, for some reason. I am curious and fascinated. I am looking to hold a much better understanding of what Angels are, and where they are. I am interested because these beings are doing God's bidding. Jesus is their leader. He's coming, and he's bringing them with Him to help carry out this second coming. This seems like a giant ordeal.

I am very tired and dissatisfied with speaking of biblical things as though it's all Folklore. I am not interested in ethereal winged creatures who float on clouds and strum harps. I don't think Hallmark in necessarily accurate in its Celestial depictions. I don't think Touched By An Angel is the gospel.

When Jesus was born, Shepherds followed a light in the sky. They were visited by an Angel, and they were very afraid. In fact, many of the people who were visited by Angels in the old days were very, very afraid. This is because they were actually visited by something they couldn't comprehend. We're talking about God's messengers. And it is written that they are coming back here with Jesus.

Angels are a big deal. Chances are when Christ gets back here, we're going to know soon enough. But no one knows when or how this is going to happen. Forgive me for considering the possibilities. Many people are content to just let God do how He sees fit. And obviously, this is what will happen. It doesn't matter if some humans speculate about it. We speculate about everything else. Why should this be different? So I admit, I speculate about how the return of our King will happen. Like a thief in the night, I've read. But what kind of thief are we talking about? A cat burgalar? A petty thief? Or is this 'heist' organized? If we're comparing our Lord and Savior to a thief, I am going to venture a guess that he's the swiftest thief of them all. I bet He's got a plan, and He knows He's going to get away with it.

It could very well be that the end of the world happens in a blink and it is all ethereal and Heaven is intangible and it's all spirits and light energy and the great mysteries of God. It's not for us to fuss about. It will happen how it happens, and that's that. There's a Book of Life. You pray. You repent. You love people. The end comes. You're in or you're out. Open and shut. Heaven and Hell. Sort us out. The end.

And if that's true, fine. Let it be. Like I've said, nothing I have written or said or thought will change it, if that's what it is. I'll just be sure to put on record that I believe in God, Jesus, and the Holy Spirit. I am a sinner. I am sorry. I wish to be saved by the amazing grace of the Holy Trinity.

PART THREE

Christian living is a pretty easy concept. Learn the Word, Believe the Word, Be the Word, Spread the Word. Jesus saves. Pass it on.

And this is enough. Nothing I do will get me into Heaven. If anything, the things I do will keep me out. I declare war on the sin in and out of me. I lose the war sometimes. And my victories are nothing to celebrate, since they fade away so quickly. The only constant here is Grace. The rest is human frailty.

What I'm getting at is none of this so far has a thing whatever to do with the Plan in action from above. You can call a coin toss in the air, and you're wrong or you're right. But the sound of your voice doesn't affect the physical laws of the toss.

Right?

So, I write what I think about the return of the King. It will have no impact on the plan in motion.

But, if you call the coin toss correctly, you gain something. You get to go first, or you get the bigger half of the doughnut. Whatever. There is a chance that I am on the right track. After all, I am using the Holy Bible to support this mission. I am relying on God to guide me. I am seeking with my heart and soul and mind. I am knocking. I am expressing my devotion to Jesus.

And honestly, I've seen the quiet and persistent faith of the Christian people who brought me into this world and raised me. Frankly, they didn't have the time or desire to break it all down and do 'mission work'. They had to do real work. Feed the children. Pay the bills. I am very lucky to live in a time and place where I can sit here and write all night about Angels and God and Jesus. I am not writing a way into Heaven. I am no more or less than the ones who put me here. It took a lot of branches in the old family tree to get me and the Bible into the same place at the same time. For this, clear back to the beginning, I am eternally grateful. Their faith is mine, and mine is theirs.

But now I'm going to start speaking freely about these thoughts that keep me awake at 5:15 am. The ones about Angels and Armageddon and Jesus' master plan to rescue His children. The heart of my little mission is to move toward that plan. I would like to do what I can to help Jesus. If this is a giant playground, He may need help with roll call. If we're scattered all over the place, maybe it would help if we got ourselves into a little line, so when He gets to us, it cuts down on confusion.

Yeah.

I'm just going to cut to the chase.

I have a hunch that when Jesus comes back, it's going to be tangible. The world is going to be able to feel Him. We're all going to get it in no uncertain terms. It's not a legend or a fabrication. It's Jesus Christ. He was a man who walked around in the sand. He was hung up on a cross by a bunch of men. His word has been spread by the mouths of human people over a span of real time and land. This is all real. Real. This is what I stress. Reality. The reality of this situation. It's so easy to forget how REAL all of this is. The world is REALLY falling to pieces. And the ideas a lot of people get about Armageddon and Angels and the Second Coming is Ethereal. Fantasy. Way out there. In a land far away. In ancient times. In the distant future. I know this because I am beating the reality of it into my own head, and still it seems so far away.

29

Maybe it's not fair to lump others in with me. Maybe the Christians today are aware in a way I am not. I am trying to make it too real, perhaps. My distinct lack of faith has driven me to cry out for something tangible. I am not satisfied to live on the quiet promises of the Holy Bible, so I seek something that simply will not be.

I concede all of this.

Doesn't change a thing. I am personally committed to searching for Angels. I am convinced that, if not in my day, than in someone's day down the line, there will be Jesus down here and it will be so real that all my speculating and cries for tangibility will be nothing at all. People will come face to face with something so incredibly alive that faith, hope, and the search of all people will combust in the light of the truth.

My theory, for the moment, is that if we get together and earnestly seek Jesus, we might come across something Divine. He's on His way. A plan of some sort is in motion. And God's messengers are commanded to work with Jesus until it is finished. A great plan usually has several steps and many phases. Just as angels were among us in the old days, so will they be in the end. Perhaps they've never left us.

Hebrews 13:2 reminds us to be kind to strangers, because maybe they're angels and we just don't know it. This is a life changing Bible verse to me. I know it may not be as big as the ones about Jesus, but I am taken by it. It inspires me every day. I can imagine...I have imagined being surrounded by angels. Knee Deep. They've got me surrounded. And I don't even know it. And I've humiliated myself over and over again. But they are patient. And they have to help me, because I've got them on a technicality: Grace. I've got this thing built into my soul that God gave me. No matter how wretched I appear to the angels, I belong to the Lord. I am like a dirty little animal that the great King has asked his servants to retrieve. I am a wanted creature, and my safe return will be greatly rewarded. I have seen ugly little dogs on posters on telephone poles. Rewards are offered every day for the safe return of the ugliest little rats. And these dogs never once say thanks, lost or found. But if I were to return a lost animal to its master, I might be rewarded. That must be the plight of some angels. To see us wretched little humans walking around, protected by grace and faith. Our sins must look particularly ugly to the Celestial. Our sin—our will was the cause of many fallen angels. A war is going on to this day over our inherent ability to do as we please.

The HOLY SPIRIT Project:
Do Not MARKET God (no satire, no ads; no irony)

You are not about to get involved in a scam.

You are not going to be tricked or duped.
You are not naïve.
You are not about to be used.

The contact you are making at this moment is real.
You have been chosen.
You are coming to a strong understanding about something big
that is inevitably happening.

This is not a game or a joke or an angle.
This is the truth, and you are a part of it.
This is for the good of mankind. This is for your own good. This
is for the future and from the past. This is an attempt to repay a
debt. Any information used for that purpose will be true and
beautiful.

This is the rest of your life.
This is not for someone else. This is not chance. This is not a
mistake.
What a time to be alive.

There is a Spirit. And this is a moment in time in which you are
alive and the spirit wants your soul to connect to it. This is your
time to connect with this spirit and let it be known that
tomorrow and every day after tomorrow is the time to get down
and understand that the world is nothing and the life upon it is
everything.

We are training.
People speak of revolutions and revelations. People speak of
safety and security.
I speak of a revolution and a revelation and of safety and of

security and it is your choice to listen or to turn away.

How will you know when God looks you in the eyes?
How will you know when you ask for a sign and He delivers it
to you with a big ribbon and a siren and a song?

What would it take for you to answer the door if God knocks
loudly and won't leave the step?

"We need a sign. Show us a sign. Where is a sign? Who can see
the signs? Will there be a sign? What sort of sign are we looking
for? Are we looking for a sign? We'd like to see a sign. Show us a
sign. We need a sign."

How's it going to end? Is it okay to wonder about how it's going
to end? Is it okay to get things in order after you know? How
about before you know?

Doomsday is a stupid word.
Prophet is a stupid word.
Fear is a horrible thing to strike in the hearts of people. Why
should we fear each other? Why should we try to scare each
other? Why is it absolutely everywhere?

Fear is all around. It's sad. But I am not here to make you afraid.
I am here to give you the strength to see the truth. Fear is
nothing compared to love, and it's about time we find some.

Love is going to have to take a stand.

I do not believe in war. There is no need to fight Fear with Love.
It's like throwing our children at the boogeyman.

It's like spitting into the ocean to change the way it tastes.

There is an ocean of fear.

You don't need to change the ocean. You need an unsinkable ship.

We can't change our oil on time. We can't save our receipts. How on earth can we change the world? How in the world can we save our souls?

I want you to become a card carrying member of the one true organization. We're getting back to the word that matters. We're getting back to basics. We're getting back to the real church. It starts today.

You are the church. You are the light. You are not a building. You are not an offering plate. You are not a weekend retreat. You are not Sunday. You are not a song. You are not a dance. You are not a memorization. You are the church.

We are taking the church into our hearts. And we are bringing the church to the people.

We are sweeping through in this day during these moments, overturning souls and glorifying God for one last opportunity to express the absolute truth.

Jesus was here. He's coming back with a plan. The plan will absolutely go into action, and the church in your heart is a part of that plan. The church belongs to the believers, and the believers are going up with Jesus in His love according to His plan and it's happening in the blink of an eye.

It happening in the end times. And what times are those? Nobody can say. Nobody knows. But what would the end times look like? What might we be capable of?

A baby was born from a virgin out in a stable. A few men followed a light in the sky to the spot where this baby was born. They were confronted by angels, and they trembled. They fell to the ground.

There were men all over the place faced with angels in dreams and visions. Lights were coming out of the sky. People saw wheels in the air. People saw angels on the sides of the road. People rose from the dead. Blind people were granted vision and crippled people walked.

We can go to the book store at any time in America today and find hundreds of books about sorcery and the supernatural and fantasy and spirituality and synchronicity and miracles and signs and marvels. There are films and digital this and that. There is music that can make the hairs on the back of our necks stand up. Goosebumps can trickle down our arms at the theater and the opera and the ballgame.

Where is the church??????
The church is stuffy on Sunday and broken into a hundred denominations and sending flyers and envelopes in the mail. The church is a commercial. The church is on the corner of this road and that street and they play bingo there on Thursday nights. I have an Aunt who's in the church choir. Our pastor moved away last year, and it hasn't quite been the same. I haven't been in there since they remodeled, but I hear it's really nice. We are camping on the weekends. We're out on business. But we'll be back. We'll come around. We're just...lazy, I guess. See our awkward smiles?

I'm a Christian. But Lutheran. Not Catholic? Not Catholic. Why not Catholic? Well, because I'm Lutheran. Not Presbyterian? Wesleyan, actually. Baptist? No, Pentecostal. Seventh-Day Adventist? What? I'm Methodist. I'm ELCA. I'm Missouri Synod. I'm a gentile. I'm a Jew. I converted. But I'm not sure. I'm agnostic. I'm non-denominational. I was baptized. I wasn't confirmed. I forgot. I'm Christian, I think. My wife is, so I am, too. I haven't been to church in a while.
 But I believe there is a God, I think.
Hmmm.....

The HOLY SPIRIT Project: Central Debriefing for the Uncertain
(Working Backwards....Clean Slate Salvation Plan)
†∞
THE HEART OF LEMNISCATE, LIVING ON EARTH, ETC.
<u>introduction to a theory, part one</u>

For some, it's easy to see that the world is a difficult and tricky place.
For some, the world is a lot of fun and life is always pretty good.
Most people try to live fun and good lives in a difficult and tricky place.

There is nothing profound to say. The world's inhabitants are young and naïve. But , when thinking about God, a few things still come to mind:

Lots of people think there's a way to get to know God better.
Lots of people have testified to the existence of God.
Lots of people think we will go somewhere else when we die.
Religion teaches about God, but also about what to do and how to be while living.
We're supposed to be good people and help each other and not hurt ourselves.
In the name of Religion, some people believe it is okay to kill people, steal land, and ruin families. But this just seems to cause a lot more problems.
Lots of people think there are good things that can happen and bad things that can happen.

These all seem like easy concepts.

World Religions deal a lot with how to behave while on earth, and what to expect in death.
But only one religion lays out a plan to save people from bad things.

We do bad things.

That is, we do things that hurt each other.
We try to control and manipulate each other.
We try pretty hard to serve ourselves as much as we can. It is
natural. But it's true. We've hurt people. People hurt us.

It is good to say to yourself now and then: Wow.
WOW.
This is all REALLY happening.
People are dying from explosions and diseases. Kids and moms
are dying of drugs and poverty and greed.

Some politicians and religious figures ARE corrupt. People ARE
liars. People ARE killing each other over shoes.

There are agencies in this world. CIA, FBI, KGB, etc.
When you join them, a great amount of knowledge is bestowed
upon you. The rest of world becomes separate from you. Many
of these societies are secret, and yet they are really happening all
around the eyes and ears of the unaware.

At this moment with these words, consider joining an agency.

introduction to a theory, part two

It is time to take all the stigmas away from this theory and
present it backwards, as though it were new. You will read
these words as though we're solving an old problem for the first
time.

The tone here is not meant to present these ideas in a harsh or
cynical way. The intention is positive.

Anyway, the first thing is this: Does Earth have a problem?
Next:
What if this problem went to an absolute extreme?

What's the worst that could happen?
Think about this. How much worse can it get?

Why, there would have to be bombs that could eradicate
countries. And diseases that could wipe out millions of people in
no time at all. There would have to be two extremes: The filthy
stinking lying rich who kill for money, and the filthy stinking
wretched poor who are dying of starvation and destitution.
Everything in the media would have to be fear-based and self
serving. It would all have to be lies, claiming to be working for
the common man, but actually working for a great, living,
breathing Beast. Everybody would have to be doing things they
hated every single day just to keep out of constant fear of losing
everything. There would need to be thousands and thousands of
terribly poisonous consumer goods that make everybody fat and
full of cancer. The most powerful nations in the world would be
a constant severe threat to the entire earth. The atmosphere
would be deteriorating exponentially. The oceans would have
filth pumped into them as quickly as humanly possible. We
would have to strip the earth of every single marketable mineral,
plant, animal, fuel, and element; we would sell all of these things
to the highest bidders and ignore all consequences. We would
all need to be lied to every single minute of every single day, age
quickly, die at the mercy of our last available currency, and pay
for the flowers on our graves.

So, when that happens...what will you do to get away?

How can anyone get away?
Can it ever get this bad?

In light of the possibility of a future emergency, there are
millions of people who believe in SAVING THE WORLD.
However, the most successful people in the most successful
countries are hard pressed to save their receipts and their
marriages.
It is difficult today to save a dolphin or give thirty cents a day

34

away to save a child in Africa.

But people campaign about saving the world.

We can build prisons. We can raise taxes. We can create drugs that slow hair loss and speed weight loss. But we can't save children from watching people kill and watching people die.

It is as awful in the world as you can imagine. And after you've imagined things to be as bad as you can, they're worse than that.

So, what do YOU seek?
Are you seeking anything?
Are you scared?

You might say:
"I seek safety.
I seek a way out.
I want a safety net."

Everywhere you look, people are preaching about safety.
Insurance. Safe Sex. Safe Driving. Safety deposit boxes. Security. Protection. Medicine. Healthcare. Freedom. Liberation.

But what might real safety be like?

Some people give practical advice about safety:
Arm yourself with the knowledge of how bad it is in our world.
Then, be really good and sensible while living.

This is probably the most practical advice.
Be good. Know bad.

But it's also impossible. There's no way to be completely good.
There's no way to know enough about evil to keep safe.

And so it seems like life is a giant trap.

So, what if God wanted to hire you to find a solution to the world's problem?

The problem is defined like this: There is no way people can be good all the time because the planet is full of bad stuff.
We run the risk of darkness taking everything over, but this possibility tends to make everyone numb. So, possibly, the whole planet could die.

We don't have to solve the problem.
You certainly don't have to solve the problem.

But, what if God did ask you or any other common person to come up with a solution?

Here are the possibilities:
We can tell each other we're going to save the planet, or we just let this planet run its course.

Who has the courage to truthfully admit there may not be a way to save the world?

Is the Earth dying? Let's consider the evidence.

What is in motion stays in motion...et cetera.

How does the following statement sit with you?: NOBODY CAN SAVE THE WORLD!!!
The things that are wrong with it have been wrong for as long as anyone can remember. The big fish eat the little ones, and we're somehow related to the fish.
Lions kill antelope.
The strong survive.
For some reason, there's an evil that totally infected this planet.
Some people do arrange this mess so that it almost looks livable.

A lot of people just wouldn't have it any other way.

So we'll just keep everything as it is.
That's how it's going to be anyway.
Nobody can agree on anything.
And all the religions can just keep going on.
We've discovered all the land.
We've decided what is of worth.
Let people buy and sell everything they can for as long as
someone's alive to buy it.

How does that sound???

Everybody who has no beef with planet earth is free to go on
living with it.

Surely, encourage people to be kind to each other whenever
possible;
Surely, encourage people not to be savage monsters.

Do for others as you would have done for you.
Or, if you prefer, do to others what has been done to you.
Is this acceptable?
What is needed then, in addition to letting the world run its
course, is an evacuation plan.
A WAY OUT OF DODGE.

So for everybody who DOES have a beef with the earth:
There should be a contingency plan.

For everybody who likes earth the way it is, let them go. Just
accept that you can't fit a square peg in a round hole.
And for anyone who is looking for something better, let there be
a contingency.

Let there be a better place to go from here.
Not earth.

Something else.

Let's make no stipulations to begin with, except that it is not earth.
Perhaps it's nicer and more fulfilling.
It would be far enough away from earth so that the people who like what's happening here won't get their hands on it.

Instead of trying to decide how things will run in the new place, let us simply discuss how to get there. Once we're there, we'll have a lot less to worry about.

So far, so good?

introduction to a theory, part three

Anyone who wants to go to the new place can just raise their hand. In deed, a show of hands. You put your hand up in the sky and say, "Yes, please. I want to leave Earth. I want to go to a better place than earth, because Earth is kind of creepy."

Yes.
You don't have to say all that. Just a simple show of hands will do.
Right on. This is simple and easy to do.

You just raise your hand. And if you have people you love who you want to take with, you make sure they raise their hands, too.
That's the first thing. Just that. Everybody who wants out, gets out.
ALL YOU HAVE TO DO IS WANT OUT.
Because, as stated previously, some people like it here. And that's their prerogative.
People have been doing whatever they've wanted to do since the beginning of mankind.
Let's be honest, and admit we cannot stop it.

But for anyone else, a simple show of hands will do. Everyone who raises their hands gets a free ticket.

That's simple enough.
Okay. Next, we'll need a way to transport everyone with their hand up.

This part seems a bit more complex. The idea about moving everyone who wants to leave earth—it seems easy enough.

But actually moving everyone?
You may have ideas about the subject. Use your imagination. There may be ways to do this.

"Analog Methods?
Digital Methods?"

Analog means to do things with real material.
Digital means to do things in code.

If we choose analog, then we need a lot of giant ships. Really amazing spaceships. They would have to hold all the people who want to leave earth. We'll need a way to contact everyone who wants a ticket, and then give them their tickets, and instruct them on how to find their ship. This will take a large scale plan. But once everyone has a ticket, and we hop on the ships, we blast off to the new place and that's that. Happily ever after, and Earth can just keep on its course.

If we choose digital, then we just realize that the entire earth is digital.
We are digital beings in a digital world. Our programming is really advanced. The graphics are really good. We take up a lot of Gigabytes. Everyone who raises their hand will be uploaded from the earth program and downloaded into a different and

better program.

These are only two strange and perhaps inconceivable ideas. Each proposes a way to get people off the earth. Each one is a possibility. We might have to put it to a vote.

This may sound crazy to many, many people. Much confusion should very practically arise about how we manage getting these fantastic ships? Or how can we expect anybody to believe that we're all digital???

It helps to discuss the real concerns in both situations.

First, there's nobody on earth who has built enough spaceships to do what is being proposed.
And nobody knows where to take us.
And nobody knows much of anything about how to arrange a worldwide network so that everyone who raises their hand can get a free ticket and hop on a ship.

In the digital scenario, we also have a few problems. Mainly, lots of people will be afraid or upset to learn that they're digital. Fifty years ago, nobody knew anything about what digital meant. Five hundred years ago, nobody knew the world was round. Even so, discovering that people are just long, long strings of ones and zeros might freak everyone out.

We do know that we're DNA.
DNA is broken down into 4 parts, designated by scientists with the letters A, T, G, and C.
If anyone interested in DNA were so inclined, they could translate DNA into digital code just like this rather effortlessly.

Scientists propose a unified theory of everything. Some say we're made of strings. Some say everything is made out tiny strings. We say for certain that life on Earth is made of DNA. One day we will theoretically be manipulating this genetic code to make life better.

We may someday have the capability to make 'digital bananas'. Ask any geneticist or computer programmer. Our genes can be made to look exactly like the Base 2 used to encode all things digital.

However, for what we know about the human genome and DNA, and for what we know about our digital capabilities, we're a long ways away from bridging the gap between our analog selves and some sort of digital universe.

Our limitations are clear. Our computers are too small. We're too primitive. And we have no ships.

So, there's just no way to rely on any human attempt to accomplish this rescue mission.

It's already a lot to ask to get us the ships or the technology needed to make us digital. But if it is possible to arrange a giant rescue for all the people with their hands up, we need even more.

What we need, of course, is an all-powerful God who can do this....

introduction to a theory, part four

I propose that there be a God who will rescue all the people who want to be saved from the dying planet Earth.

God can rescue us via spaceships, by digital means, or however He sees fit.

That way, God can have the big computers and know the big program. God can do all the uploading and downloading.

Or, God can build all the ships and find us all with a giant worldwide network.

God can figure out the details. The point is, it's beyond human capability.

But if we're going to proceed with any of these ideas, we're going to have to consider some sort of all-powerful God. God will have created everything, so that only God can save us.

God will create a worldwide network. Whether we're saved digitally or with ships or however it happens, there just needs to be a system in place that gives God ultimate and unlimited access to everything.
God's network should be present, and it should have always been here...ever present since humans were but a glimmer of the eye.

We'll leave the details up to God. The point is, there is a God, and there is a real live digital/analog network. And with this network, God will be able to see whose hands are in the air when the big rescue mission happens.

Perhaps God should be able to use the network for other things. Things like working miracles.
Things like introducing people to each other, and tying up all sorts of loose ends while arranging the rescue mission.
This network cannot be so cumbersome that it interferes with the people who want nothing to do with it.
It may drive certain people insane to know that a network is controlling everything.
So God can just reserve this network for the people who are at peace with the idea that it is real.

So, let there be God and a giant plan, and a giant network to help God with the plan.

Still, we need one more thing...

<u>introduction to a theory, part five</u>

We need a way to make sure everybody knows about what's

going to go down.

EVERYBODY. We can't have a giant rescue mission unless we're sure that everyone who wants off earth can get off earth.

All for one and one for all.
Do for others as you'd have it done for you.

But we can't just let God yell it out at everybody.
That would upset the people who don't want to have anything to do with the network and the rescue plan.

And this cannot simply be a theory or a creative idea. It cannot be proposed by science or art.
It would never fly. People are not capable of this salvation work.

REALITY CHECK:

Ask yourself the following: If you could truly know that all this was set up and about to happen...suppose it's happening in a few weeks, or a few months. You raise your hand, and God knows it, so you get a ticket and so does everyone you care about who raises their hands. You have some sort of inside information. Like this text. The text you are reading, at this moment....suppose this is the absolute key to salvation. Suppose there is a ticket on the last page of this text. Suppose this ticket is redeemable for exiting this world, and you will absolutely go to a better place. No gimmicks, no games. Real action.
God and His network has brought this text to your attention to pose these extremely important questions. Are you willing to raise your hand? Are you willing to go away from here to live in a new place created by God for you?

This is not a fairy tale. This is not a game. Really, really imagine this. You blast off. You go to the next place.

If you're not willing to consider this, then maybe you're happy.

Maybe there's no need for you to be part of the rescue mission. That's okay. It's all up to you.

This is not an attempt to ask whether or not you personally **believe or suppose** it could happen. It's a step beyond that. This is an attempt to explain that your belief does not matter. You should decide within yourself if you're willing to go away, given you were ABSOLUTELY GUARANTEED a ticket.

People have a lot of complaints about life on Earth. But some people do not.

As for the plan, this text is an introduction to something gigantic and amazing. It's about a rescue mission from Earth. And it rests on the shoulders of a single ambassador...

introduction to a theory, part six

We need a spokesperson. However, he or she can't be political or religious. This person has to be common, and has to be someone everybody can deal with.

We need an ambassador who will see to it that everyone knows God is rescuing people of the world who have raised their hands.
Everyone must know there is a plan and everyone who raises their hand will be included.

So, this person will have to come directly from God.
Completely Authentic.
This ambassador cannot be threatening or someone to be afraid of. God should make this ambassador human, made of our own flesh and blood. Let God send us a human being as an ambassador.

If this ambassador is going to be a woman or a man, there should be no sex scandals. If this ambassador stays completely out of the sexual arena, gender would not matter. Divisions created by human opinion about the ambassador's gender must be averted. These concerns would make for a less authentic extension of God's willingness to rescue humanity.

If he's a man, he'll have to have a really wonderful mother, so that everyone will respect him and his mom.

Everyone will have to know that he's actually God's spokesman. But, he can't accomplish this with commercials or political campaigning or anything earthly.

He should not get rich while he's presenting his message, and he should not be given royal treatment. His message is too important to be clouded by earthly ambitions.

All he's got to do is tell everyone to raise their hands when they want to leave earth. It's simple. He doesn't need anything else. He needs an easy, understandable message.

He can't get caught up in any sort of scandal, or the message will be lost.

In short, he can't do anything wrong at all.

He only does good things. Nothing bad. If he comes from God, he should be able to go around here telling us how to leave earth, and not do anything wrong.

And even better, if he's from God, he should be able to do really amazing things that only God can do.

This spokesman for God is going to let everyone know to raise their hands and get off earth, so we need to find a way for every single person in the whole world to hear his message.

Since this man is going to be human, he won't live nearly long enough to tell everyone himself. There's just no way.

So, we'll ask him to choose a crew to help him.

They should follow him around, befriend him, and hear what he has to say.

They should be from different walks of life, so we get many

perspectives.

Their accounts should be written and saved for reference.

Then, between God, the giant network, and us, we'll distribute the news about him to EVERYONE.

That means the publication--the news about the ambassador-- has to be the most popular book in the world. It has to top all the charts for sales, distribution, and everything else.

It should be available EVERYWHERE.

This is one man's story about THE plan to save everybody who wants to be free of Earth.

This must be emphasized: this publication of good news should be the largest message on Earth.

It's a simple message: just raise your hand and get saved—but the distribution of this message needs to be the biggest news distribution on earth.

Not everyone needs to like it or accept it or make a huge deal out of it, but everyone has to know about it.

The rescue mission can happen when everyone has had a fair shot to put up their hand.

The story about the man has to be pretty good, too. If he's boring, people might ignore the story. And since we're dealing with God's own messenger, here, we might as well make it so that everybody understands what exactly is happening.

So the ambassador has to be ordinary, like I said, but also the direct descendent of God. It should be as thought God Himself touches down on Earth to tell us about the rescue He is planning.

He'll get followed around by people who he hires to tell his story.

He goes around doing miracles and getting people to think about why it might be a good idea to leave earth someday.

He can talk about the good things to do on earth and the bad things.
But he's not a hypocrite or fake – so he can't do anything wrong.

However, we don't want his message to bring shame to everybody.
He has to understand that here on earth, everybody makes mistakes.
He may be perfect, but humans are not.
He is only here to announce the rescue mission.

He'll have to tell everyone to be good, and that being evil just makes everything on earth worse.
He'll have to make sure humanity knows that he's absolutely carrying out the rescue mission.
He'll say that everyone who believes in what he's talking about, RAISE THEIR HANDS, and they will most definitely be saved.

introduction to a theory, part seven

This plan is going to raise a few issues with the general public.
One of them is pretty obvious: Why does all this have to happen? What makes it fair?
What gives God the right to do all this?
There are a lot of problems on earth. Really bad things happen to really good people.
And NOBODY gets through without doing at least a few things wrong, so why live like this?
Even with worldwide rescue from the dying planet, why is there a dying planet to begin with? Some people are grateful, but most people are upset about the injustice of this place. And some people might be so angry that they don't think a rescue mission is enough to make right all that's wrong with the world.

God's only ambassador will say everything will be all right if we all just raise our hands, but how can he justify this in the

presence of the dark and evil misery and hardship on earth?
There is only one thing to do. This ambassador and this message
must be compelling enough to stand against all the darkness in
the world.

Even though this man is a saint speaks only of a way out, he
should be willing to die at the hands of the people on earth.
People who are angry or think they're better than God will do
their worst. And everyone who hears about him will know his
death is as bad it gets.
Then no one can say God doesn't understand the pain involved
in living. If God is alive in this man, he'll surely know the pain
we all go through.

And when this man is dying, he'll have to hold true to his
message.

This story will give God credibility.
It will touch and sadden the people on earth, if they have a heart
left at all.
And the truth is, humanity doesn't deserve this mission and this
spokesman.

If this plan works, people would give God their hearts for what
is done just to save those who put their hands in the air.

Humans who wish to leave Earth should not desire the next
place to become another problem-ridden Earth. These problems
should not follow humanity.
So, in hope of a better place:

Don't carry your mistakes to the next place. Don't leave Earth
just to corrupt the next place. Let go. Take a stand against the
things in your life that are wrong.
Be prepared to look into the eyes of the ones you love, and admit
your faults.
Celebrate the life in you and abandon the death in you.

When the time comes to be free of our sorrow, consider it a good thing.

Until then, be aware of your mistakes. It's the only way to improve. If you're not sorry for being bad, you'll be taking it where ever we go next.

In the new place, *nobody needs your strife*.

That being said, distribute the spokesman's pledge.
This will be a huge job.
It will have a name. Our ambassador will have a name.
It could be any name.
Any name will do.
The name's not important. The rescue mission is important.
What's important is knowing what the spokesman said and what he did.
It's saying to yourself,
"I want to be saved from this place, and he's making it happen."

Then, when everyone knows about the plan, and has decided whether or not they'll put their hand in the air, he'll come back and get everybody. God and the giant network will go into motion and the plan to rescue everyone will get going.

Is it by ship? Is it by code? Is it by light?

However it is to be, God will see us through it all.

So, it's a pretty simple plan.
The bases are covered.
The people who want to stay on earth can do so freely and keep on worshiping whoever and whatever they want.
And all the people who want to leave earth and this way of life can do so. Some people are going to resent the ambassador and the story, because people seem to have problems with everything that comes along.

CONCLUSION of this theory:

Between these three things:

God, the entity responsible for making everything and everyone
And
God's Ambassador, who is God and man, and tells us how we're getting out of here and dies to prove it's the justifiable truth
And
God's giant network, that connects everyone and facilitates miracles in our lives, and reveals the ambassador to the entire world

Between these **three** entities, there's a framework for saving people from themselves.

Solving the problems of the world would require something as grand as this.

Will your hand go up?

If only there were such a plan.
If only there were such a thing as a rescue mission and a giant network and God and an ambassador.
If only there were a publication which talked about all of this, and was indeed the largest of all publications.
If only...
Wouldn't that be great if there were such a thing?
†∞
(Like the CIA and the FBI, there are many agencies in this world.
A very exciting part of life is knowing there is more than what you imagine.
In times like these, it is difficult to consider that the next stranger you meet is an angel, or that the next book you pick up contains the sign you're searching for.
Some people believe in a rescue mission like the one outlined above.

Some people know more about it than others.

Is your hand up?
If you want a ticket out of here, start considering the methods in which God would get your ticket to you. After all, it isn't going to spit out of an ATM.

Faith means more than you might think.
It is through Faith that you find your ticket.
If you're looking for a sign that GOD wants to get you out of here:

`<yield>`

This IS a sign. You're reading THIS. It's no mistake.
If you would like to know more about the agency responsible for helping those whose hands are raised, contact God directly through prayer. You will be notified. The network is in place, and the agency is thriving.)

It's good to say to yourself sometimes,
WOW. This is really happening...

* 9 7 8 1 3 1 2 9 2 1 7 9 5 *